D1029790

Ella Sue
and the
Burlap
Bag

Robin Taylor-Chiarello
Illustrated by Steven Lester
Edited by Marion Davidson

the Peppertree Press
Sarasota, Florida

About Ella Sue

Ella Sue Hartgrove (Brewton)

Ella Sue Hartgrove, the daughter of sharecroppers Jessie and Estelle Hartgrove, was born in Shelby, North Carolina. She is a proud North Carolinian and enjoys recounting the stories about her youth and family. As an adult, Ella Sue moved north with her three children to enjoy educational opportunities for them, and higher wages for herself. Ella Sue loves visiting the Shelby area and seeing relatives and friends while enjoying worshipping at her old church. She believes that faith, family, and prayer are the most important components to a good life. She sends her blessings to you.

Dedications

The story of Ella Sue is dedicated to all of the children
who help their families during challenging times.
May they always remember, through determination
and resilience, comes clarity and brilliance.

— Robin Taylor Chiarello

and

To Billy Ray and Timothy, my wonderful brothers,
that were born later in my life.

— Ella Sue Hartgrove (Brewton)

I was born in Shelby a long time ago.

My parents were sharecroppers and worked with a hoe.

The farmland they managed had a
Plank House and fields.

The crops would produce all the food for our meals.

Beef we purchased at the Blanton's Store.

Our life was good, we didn't want more.

I passed my sixth birthday so now it is fine,
to help my family during cotton picking time.

When the picking is right, the days are long.
Your work is hard, you must be strong!

Daddy will soon give me a tan burlap bag. It stands tall as me with my name on a tag.

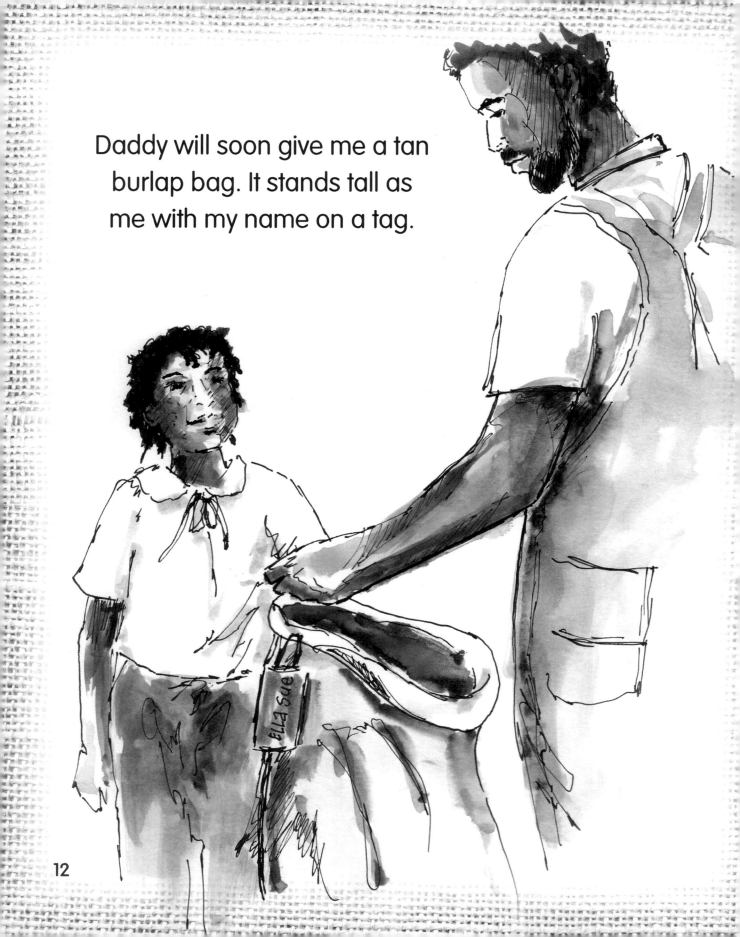

"Ella Sue, it is time for you to help in the fields.
We work as a family, it helps pay for our meals."

My parents were kind with love in their eyes.
When they asked for your help you knew not to cry.

Momma and Daddy work very hard.
Sisters Lois and Helen tend the barnyard.

Brother William feeds chickens, a cow and a lamb.
I'm old enough now to give them a hand.

William stocks the root cellar under the house.
Veggies stay cool under the watch of a mouse.

My family heads out to the long cotton rows,
mud under my feet comes up through my toes.

To work in the field means we must miss school.
Come mid-October, that's Daddy's rule.
Not all my classmates have to pick.
They don't spend their day getting itchy and pricked.
These soft little hands get cut as I go.
There is no fast way to do this, just take it row by row.

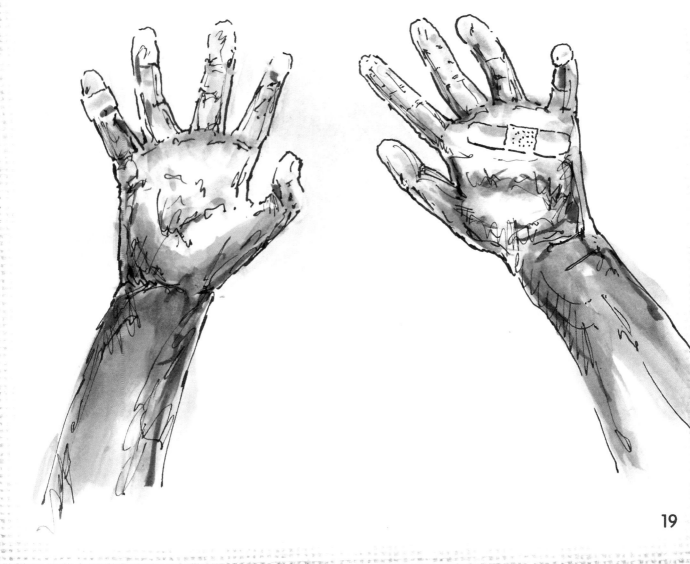

Day after day I must fill my bag.
By the 4th week of picking it is starting to drag.

Momma's at the Plank House with soup simmering away.
We all leave the fields, to eat at mid-day.

When the harvest is finished, and my bag's emptied out,
it will come home for a scrubbing to be washed and
dried out. Hung on the clothesline, softened by sun,
made into a dress, it's my very first one!

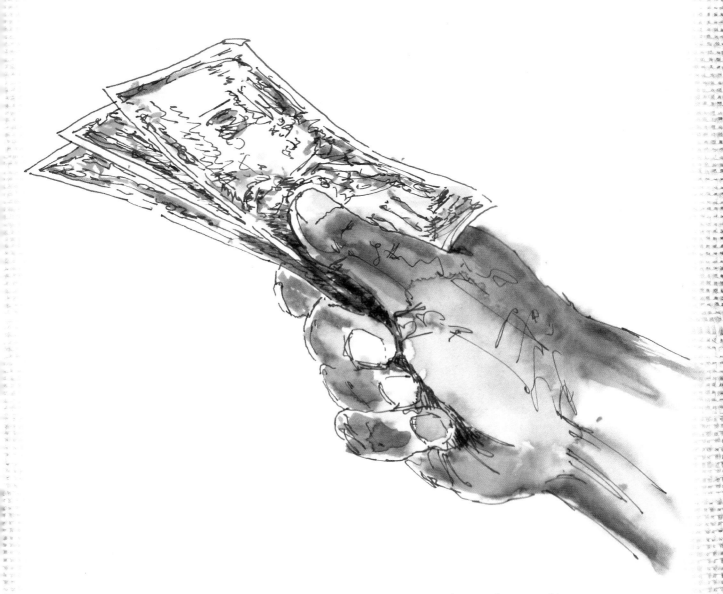

Mr. Shorty Specs manages our land. He'll soon
be here, and put out his hand. There will be dollar bills,
and twenties too, to pay my Daddy for the work that we do.
He brings burlap bags filled with grains and seeds,
grits and rice, and all that we need.

I give Momma a
hug for my new
burlap dress.
It's a new look…
upgraded from
my usual mess.

Barrettes, some ribbons, and bows in my hair,
I'll wear them to church and treat them with care.

A knock, knock, knock loud sounds at the door.
It's a man with a package from Miss Rosie's store.

He gives us a smile and turns with a twirl.
It's a bag of saddle shoes for the three Hartgrove girls!

I know some people will think that it's odd.
We walk two miles every Sunday to pray to our God.

The little white church on the green grassy hill,
saying prayers, sharing friendship, it's always a thrill.

When the preacher gets finished we all bow our heads.
Thank God for our harvest and pray over our bread.

The Deacon's wife treats us to a large picnic ham.
Chicken and gravy and a helping of yams.

We sing songs, play games, for an hour or two.
Sundays for families is a time to renew.

My burlap dress lets my church members know,
I'm big enough now to work with a hoe.
It gives me great joy to help Mom and Dad.
If you can't help your family, life would be very sad.

Blessings to you
from Ella Sue